ab•nor′mally HAPPY

A GAY DICTIONARY

by Richard Summerbell
illustrated by Paul Aboud

Text © 1985 by Richard Summerbell
Illustrations © 1985 by Paul Aboud

First printing October 1985
1 2 3 4 5 89 88 87 86 85

Canadian Cataloguing in Publication Data

Summerbell, Richard Charles, 1956-
   Abnormally happy

ISBN 0-919573-41-X

1. Homosexuality - Anecdotes, facetiae, satire, etc.
I. Aboud, Paul, 1955-   II. Title.
PN6231.H57S85 1985   306.7'66'0207   C85-091528-7

The publisher is grateful to the Canada Council for assistance provided through the Writing and Publication Section.

New Star Books Ltd.
2504 York Avenue
Vancouver, Canada   V6K 1E3

Printed and Bound in Canada

with insincerest apologies to Ambrose Bierce (and dedicated to Ross)

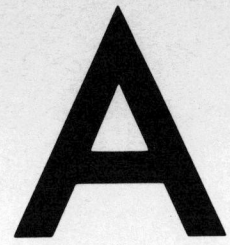

abnormal
1. Threatening to established interests. 2. Virtually unknown in Silage County, Iowa, on the morning of June 3, 1946.

abstractions
The muddled, idealistic concepts propounded by one's opponents — bearing no resemblance, of course, to the murky messianic shibboleths one has embraced oneself.

JUNE 4, 1946: AT FIRST, FRED THOUGHT IT WAS JUST SELMA'S CHICKEN DINNER NOT SETTING RIGHT.

ABNORMAL

aesthetics
The "gay sensibility," as understood by academics.

alcoholic
Person who can drink his or her own worst enemy under the table.

antique shop
Business catering to those who spare no pretense in obtaining the right decor.

apolitical
In favour of the status quo.

Art (gay)
Two thousand excellent conceptual pieces and 42,659,545 phalli.

atheism
The belief that God (or Goddess) should be replaced by a committee.

"attitude"
A belief in the reality of one's artificiality. That portion of a person's attributes which naturally appeals to the Madame Tussaud in each of us. In bars, often the equivalent of wearing a "keep off the grass" sign — a thing particularly resented by those looking for a "roll in the hay."

authority
In business, that which allows one to disperse the daily dunghill among the appropriate beetles. In volunteer organizations, that which permits the beetles to make one the nucleus of an ever-enlarging dung ball.

avowed homosexual
A gay nun or priest.

B

B&D
"Bonds and Discipline," an S/M scenario in which one tortures one's partner by threatening to invest all his or her money at 4% per annum.

back room
A small, enclosed park lacking bushes.

bagel
An organic cockring.

bar
To many gay men, a place where you go to drink until you get picked up — either by a man, or off the floor.

bawdy house
In Canadian law, a place where two or more individuals in official disfavour have sex.

bigot
One who invests his sense of personal worth in the arbitrary. A toad who believes that the essence of mortal splendour lies in the possession of warts.

If some folk have improper skins,
it follows, then, that some folk own
the finest skin, the skin that wins
the prizes with its perfect tone.
If some folk have improper love
it seems that others must with ease
accomodate to proper love,
correct despite deficiencies
— such that even if love turns to
war, a Punch and Judy show,
it still by its correctness earns
great virtue in its every blow.
And so it goes with skins and sex,
this narcissistic comedy:
the "rednecks" get their rosy necks
by blushing at "indecency"—
their own indecent Vanity!

— **Ignatius Digg**

bisexuality

Attribute possessed by everybody, by nobody, or by some people. Utopia or limbo. In some cases, a learner's licence for homosexuality. Bisexuality is often thought to be something to aspire to by individuals who would never consider broadening their tastes within the sex of their initial preference.

boot

In some segments of the S/M community, a pedal lollipop. Thanks to the wonders of modern marketing, boots now come in flavours other than the original licorice.

BOOT

boredom
The most dangerously contagious of the non-venereal diseases.

breasts
The author lacks expert knowledge on this subject and has had to poll certain indiscreet friends:

Pillows that let you know when they like you.
— **Melanie Blanchette**

Sort of like chocolate-coated sundaes where you never feel guilty about going for the cherry first!
— **Luinda Ndebe**

Essential objects which keep the bra from shimmying down the torso.
— **Etheldora Duncan, author of** Underwear: Naked Clothing — A Satirical Dictionary

My mom and her girlfriend call them "huggy bumpers."
— **Melissa M.,** *age 4*

A child's first fast-food outlet.
Melissa's mom

Speaking strictly for myself, volcanoes rising out of a sea of lust. Don't print that.
— **Georgina M. Smith-Jones**

breeder
Epithet referring to any active heterosexual, as: "Unfortunately, I descend from an unbroken line of breeders."

brunch
The true home of the pomegranate-and-sweet-potato omelette. Eggs over easy and hash brown potatoes are never brunch, no matter what time of day they are served.

buns
Confections of muscle; not to be confused with "rolls," which are confections of fat.

butch
Macho with a purse. The mental equivalent of a false moustache.

CELIBACY

C

capitalism
The inverted tree-of-all-evil in which the "root of all evil" is concentrated at the top. Leaves below are subject to seasonal layoff.

celibacy
Fulfillment of a vow to hide one's own sexual activity.

chicken
Term of envy referring to a male person who has no stubble the morning after.

child molester
A paedophile with long, green fingers.

children
Young, small human beings, used by some heterosexuals as a means of publicly flaunting their sexual proclivities.

circumcision
Among WASPs, an act of sanitation and good health, much like removing the face in order to prevent acne. Among Jewish men, a religious act unwittingly ministering to the needs of those who write intimate classified ads.

civil rights
An official recognition that a minority contains a substantial number of voters.

climax
The Big Bang. In youth, this matchless event may give rise to an ever-expanding universe of romantic expectation. Alternatively, it may resolve itself in a inestimable number of "black holes."

clones
Those who do not affect the mannerisms of chic nonconformists.

closet
Basement suite of a heterosexual outhouse.

cock
Device marking "North" on the human male compass. The smokestack of the male imagination. A microphone with which one's friend(s) can broadcast directly to the Interior. A decanter for the sociable urges. Also, unfortunately, a one-lane viral superhighway.

collective
Committee with permission to bicker.

colony
Foreign territory acquired by those proceeding aboard ship. Foreign territory acquired on foot is not referred to as a "colony," but as a "socialist republic."

Community Centre, Gay
Homosexual Kingdom Hall.

consent
Transaction in which one deliberately and independently says "yes" to another's proposal. Knowledgeable consent: consent given with full knowledge of the implications of the decision, i.e., that consent which none of us save the prophets are qualified to give.

conservatism
The belief that your own constant complaints are valid, unlike those of troublemakers, shit-disturbers, and rabble-rousers.

couple-ism
The destructive myth that two people can get along together.

Crisco
Bare-grease.

CRUISING

cruising
A reckless act often leading to the collision of two humans of similar make and model.

cum
The adult or adolescent's foremost emission in life. For men, the lusty spouting of a whale-of-a-good-time. For women (or so I'm told) the rainbow of gold at the end of the pot.
"Frottage cheese."
— Ebenezer Burfe, *Why We Should Ban Sex*

custody
Lease to rent a child from the adult it will become. When in dispute, this is usually awarded to whichever of two parents most pleases an unbiased, opinionated ex-lawyer.

daycare
A danger to society, unlike babysitters, nursery schools, kindergartens, and elementary schools.

dear
Among men, a term of affectionate disdain for someone who momentarily appears more foolish than the speaker.

DEAR

desire
An emotion with sticky fingers. An organic "gimme." Take note, though: left-wingers, in their moral supineness, labour under the sway of sexual and emotional "needs." Only right-wingers, in their self-deluding vaingloriousness, restrict themselves to the possession of "desires." Members of the latter group, however, lie prostrate and panting in the boudoirs of capital, while members of the former group grimly repress any perverse fiscal lusts which should happen to descend upon them. And never the twain shall meet.

deterrence
The theory that one keeps dogs from fighting by supplying them with longer teeth.

deviant (*adj.*)
Objectively heretical.

deviant (*n.*)
A person who wanders from the One True Path and is caught urinating somewhere in the midst of the unthinkable. A person taking any exit ramp off the freeway of self-righteousness.

disco
A series of thumps with orchestral backing. Inexplicably, it has been associated by homophobes with the horrors of oral sex (— sucks).

discreet
Completely lacking discernible gay characteristics; beyond suspicion, like Liberace. Not being so tactless as to make the self-evident obvious. Alternatively, avoiding undue personal display, as: "Discreet, straight-looking gay guy wishes to walk down the street holding hands with same."

dogma
Uncompromising statements of principle or belief, as: "People don't grow up — they just begin to overestimate their own importance," or "It is not sufficient to have compassion only for those who are cute."

drag
Female impersonation. Consists largely of a thick layer of make-up through which stubble inexorably penetrates. The obscure sport of drag-racing is still practised in some areas. In this sport, a race is won by the person who can run the farthest without smearing make-up.

drugs
Illicit substances which arouse suspicion by causing ordinary citizens to look and act like the hosts of religious television shows.

energy
Affection or liking. To "have no energy for" is to disapprove of.

equality
The recognition that we all feel equally superior to one another.

erotica
The depiction of naked men. Depictions of naked women are far less innocent and are known as "pornography."

EROTICA (PORNOGRAPHY)

estie
Colloquial for "EST trainee." A born-again capitalist.

etiquette
A collection of high-camp dramas scripted for dinner parties or coy conversations. These inventive rites have unfortunately been taken up by pedants and parents, who prefer that the champagne of etiquette be served flat.

faggot
Gay owner of a woodburning stove.

fag hag
Anti-gay term directed at heterosexual women. This term cleverly allows the user to express homophobia by proxy. In many cases, the so-described woman's only crime is having done a superior job of female impersonation. At least a few women, however, really do possess a desire to have sex with gay men — even at the price of having to acquire a supply of butt plugs and/or opera recordings.

faith healing
The art of making irreversibly handicapped people feel guilty about their faithlessness.

family
1. The combination of parents and their children. 2. A sacred institution, staunchly defended by Southern Baptists, Mormons, and Mafiosi. Meaning 2 is not to be confused with meaning 1.

fanatic
An Anti-American with Asian, Latin, or Semitic features.

fem
Hobgoblin much-feared by writers of classified ads. The fem is believed to appear as the mirror image of the ad-writer, except that it is wearing full drag. It mesmerizes its victim and carries him home in a sack made of pantyhose.

feminism
The first movement which, when fully successful, will not go down in the history of Mankind. At present, an uphill struggle.

Teach all your daughters, and every son
what pride we've earned, what rights
   we've won;
then rest an hour, whilst sets the sun:
a feminist's work is never done...
— **Virginia Coyotte**

fisting
A revisionist interpretation of the old adage, "the way to a man's heart is through his stomach." Some people say fistfucking is a real extension of our sexual frontiers; others maintain that it is merely a blind alley.

foreplay
Sex before going to the theatre together.

free enterprise
Insidious political advertising slogan created by businessmen who found they could always attract customers to their stores by putting up signs which said "Free! Enter! Prize!"

Said businessman to doctor,
"It's free enterprise for me,
a system of incentives
and a strong economy.
Although I'm now unwell, I've
lived more productively
than welfare bums and beggars—
who deserve no sympathy."
"I'm sure you're right," said Medic,
"it's incentive people need:
the prospect of the poorhouse,
the hungry kids to feed;
and you, you need incentive
to correct your present ills.
Please make yourself a healthy man—
I'm cutting off your pills!"
— **Engelbert Friedrichs**

French
An act so named by the English because it makes proper pronunciation difficult.

gay
Abnormally happy.

gay liberation
Militants engaged in a wicked attempt to beleaguer gays into abandoning their most basic principles of self-abasement.

gay rights
Human rights casting a bugaboo's shadow. According to the right wing, gay rights are always achieved at the expense of someone else's rights. For example, some conservative heterosexual men are fearful that gay rights abrogate their own right not to have to worry about wearing a strategically-placed cork.

gentle
In life, non-warlike. In sex, bambisexual.

I met a bambisexual
a cuddly-wuddly lad.
He cuddled some, and wuddled all
the rest, and said, "I'm glad."
He further said, "I like the kind
of man who favours hugging.
Tis more to my own taste, I find,
than balls with chains a-tugging.
My gentle man likes true romance
and tea on sunny morns,
and if by chance he picks a rose
he doesn't wear the thorns."
— Wilbur Wimplegon

ghetto
A cluster of two or more businesses serving gays.

GHETTO

girl
A man of any age.

good friend
Memento of a deceased relationship.

gossip
A method by which many of us fulfill the Golden Rule.

Greek
One-upmanship in its most equitable form. Whether one is "one-up" or "one-upped" is, of course, a matter of taste. In the passive form, this is an act which can reveal the exact degree of one's passion — provided that the appropriate thermometer is correctly in place.

GWM
"Gay White Masturbator" — a person so pale and desperate that he resorts to classified advertising.

gym
Sweat without love.

herb
Plant which stimulates the imagination.

herstory
Much more, we now know, than just a collection of old wives' tales. Despite right-wing accusations to the contrary, also more than just a collection of old non-wives' tales.

HECK, FRANCINE! WE COULD GET US A HOUSE AND MOVE TO THE SUBURBS!

HETEROSEXUALITY

heterosexuality
That which impels one to move to the suburbs.

highbrow
A neanderthal on a pedestal.

history
Scandal warmed over. A repository of famous justifications for being pro-lesbian and pro-gay.

Children, Whitman wasn't gay—
he just took men to bed.
"We're just good comrades," he would say,
"I hope you're not misread;
for when two men lie arm-in-arm
their thoughts become complex
but with a woman, there'd be harm:
'twould lead, I fear, to sex!"
— **Muriel Cubberd**

homophile
One who collects homosexuals, or who esteems fine homosexuals of good vintage.

homophobia
The unreasoning fear of homogenized milk. This neurosis extends to the fear of a society which is not vertically stratified in the manner of whole milk.

homosexual
A being endowed by some with superhuman powers of destroying moral fibre. According to legend, moral fibre was pressed from hemp until homosexuals discovered that the plant could be smoked.

human being
A gay person who does not wish to be thought of as gay.

hustler
An independent youth earning more than the minimum wage.

The perils of a hustler's life
may climax in an early grave,
but still, I'll never know the strife
of being a McBurger slave.
— **Hustler's Working Song**

I

icon
A small *objet d'art* signifying the presence of the deity; e.g., a gilt painting for the Orthodox Greek, or a $50 bill for the TV fundamentalist.

immoral
Obsolete expression meaning "politically incorrect."

INVERT

increasing
Not decreasing in the manner desired. Alternatively, new to the cognizance of the speaker, as: "When I was in the crib there were no homosexuals around. Now, increasingly, they are everywhere."

intelligence
The ability to be convincingly pretentious.

invert
Upside-down homosexual. There are many inverts south of the equator.

journalism
The art (or science) of expressing life as a series of cliches.

KKK

K

KKK

Ferocious, stupid race distinguished by skin colour, specifically a red hue of neck. Some 3-K's have an embarrassing tendency to bite out or shoot off their own freckles and moles. Others have become unhinged when confronted with bagels. They often put forth the claim that Jesus Christ was born in a Louisville mobile home park. In this version Christ, the son of a humble gunsmith, went to Palestine to arouse antisemitism among the Romans, but later chose to commit suicide after being labelled "King of the Jews." KKKs produce offspring, and to the extent that children resemble their parents, these nitwits can be thought of as a sexually-transmitted disease.

lady
A woman propped up on pedestal heels and polished to a high-gloss sheen. Glitz and bric-a-brac with dignity.

leader
The flimsy, barely visible, nylon line which secures a baited fishhook; hence, a human being who dangles a political promise of any kind.

LADY

leather
Material used in the manufacture of clothing. It is noted for causing the human exterior to resemble that of a bald cow.

lesbian
According to legend, a person who is distinguished from a truck driver only by her vastly smaller income. In real life, a person who incurs the wrath of many men simply by being independent.

Though she's often seen in skin magazines
the lesbian feels estranged
from a system that only lets women
   make love
when their limbs are man-arranged.
— **Vidalia Sapphoon**

lesbian woman
The female analogue of the gay male man.

liberal
One who uses forked tongue to lightly tickle objects of condescension on both sides of the status quo. This action may be used to distract opponents from the fact that the liberal is liberally helping him- or herself to their money.

libertarian
A dismantler of government influence on the economy. In general, someone who is uncomfortably aware that money does not vote.

libertarian (left-wing)
One who believes that humanity might be led to freedom if only people had the courage to go where their erotic impulses led them. In men, the process of finding freedom would somewhat resemble dowsing.

lint
A constant and irksome reminder of humanity's fallen state — when one considers that Adam and Eve began life lacking both clothing and belly-buttons. The profound metaphysical significance of lint has yet to be given due consideration by fundamentalist theologians.

lisp
An unnecessarily sibilant pronunciation of the common English word "lithp." Lithping is most common among speakers of Castilian Spanish (Ethpanol), all of whom have had strong mothers and weak fathers, or authoritarian fathers and weak, clinging mothers.

love
For some, lust putting on its best Sunday suit. For others, a thing as heartwarming as a pink bunny nibbling on a plastic flower. In a heterosexual context, love may be symbolized by a very small piece of real estate, generally a diamond, which serves to represent the couple's resolve to mortgage a much larger piece of ground. Even in its most transcendent state, love is a Houdini which must continually escape the strongbox of cliche. It succeeds in doing so only because it, like its adherents, is completely irrational.

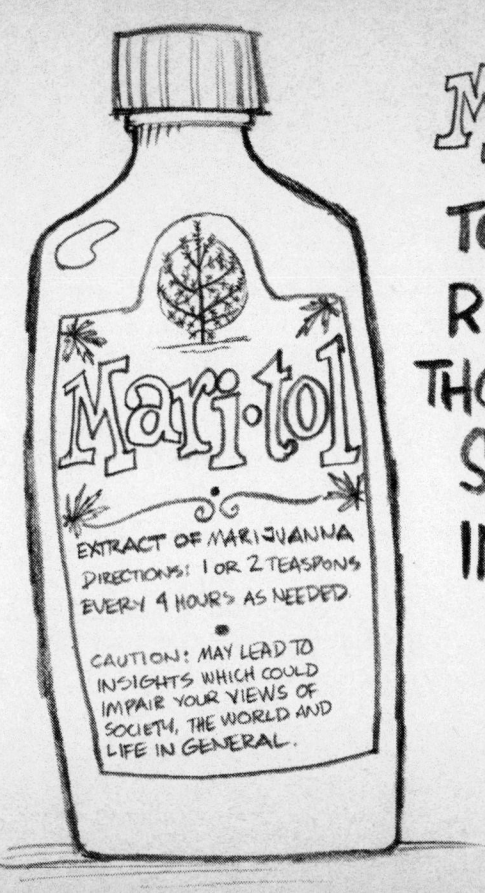

MARIJUANA

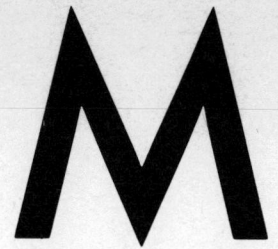

macho
The sound of a sneeze billowing through a heavy moustache.

marijuana
The Geritol of adolescence.

Marxism
The philosophy which teaches that all oppression arises from the capitalist class structure, with the exception of the oppression of gays, women, religious groups, national minorities, artists, and workers in Marxist countries.

mellow
As unflappable as the wings of a dodo. The emotion of human turtles who do not yet realize they have no shells.

militant
Determined; not easily daunted; as, "The child was born after two hours of militant labour unrest."

missionary position
An unnatural sex act, belly-to-belly, not practiced by beast, fish, fowl, or tree.

modern
Neo-mundane.

monogamy
Sexual macrobiotic diet and/or sexual manna. Morally legislated obsessiveness and/or state of grace. Primarily known among geese; claims of discovery amongst certain groups of Baptists is unsubstantiated at present. Only known evidence: bumper stickers which say, "Honk if you love Jesus."

morality
To conservatives, the philosophical underpinnings of the quest for More.

Mormonism
Religion which beatifies reproduction and uses beehive as its symbol. Unfortunately, 99% of bees are non-reproductive.

moustache
The nasal insignia of a policeman. In ordinary mortals, a gadget used for removing the lint from other men's moustaches.

movement
As in "The Movement": An often-directionless milling activity participated in by large numbers of idealists. Often stimulates internecine combat.

narcissist
One who fails to pay sufficient attention to *me*.

New Right
God's wolves-in-sheep's-clothing.

normality
Hypothetical characteristic ascribed to people inhabiting particularly monotonous utopias. This term can also be used by any individual who wishes to describe the essence of his or her own nature.

nuclear power
Electricity for nuclear families.

OPERA

opera
Highbrow kitsch. A pink plastic flamingo on the lawn of classical music.

order
Chaos saluting itself. Order, like chaos and all conditions in between, is an inexaustible wellspring of human grief. Civilizations march back and forth between order and disorder like miserable wolves pacing in a second-rate zoo.

organization
An institution named after its most fervent and futile hope.

P

passive
In straight sex, active while lying on your back. In gay sex, disporting a paler shade of leather jackboots than your partner. (Or some such thing.)

patriarchy
System in which human worth is proportional to the fresh weight of external genitalia. A society run along the lines of a delicatessen meat counter, where the "wurst" is always best. The absolute rule of a phallacy.

peace
A condition unknown on earth, but certain to follow a nuclear war.

people
As in "The People": That part of a population which reflects the self-interests of its leaders. Not to be confused with the "silent majority," which is the illusory dummy used by ambitious political ventriloquists.

Perrier
A mechanism by which cultural superiority can be swallowed.

perverse
Employing rhyming poetry as a means of romantic entreaty.

A Tennyson or Blake you're not!—
Few poets could be worse:
In sex, you are persistent, but
In love, you are per-verse!
— **The Virgin George**

poker
Male organ. Term is used primarily in lavender-shaded purple prose. Synonyms: rod, tool, hotrod, spanner, torque wrench, butterfly nut, drainpipe.

poodle
A high-camp hairstyle imposed on an otherwise undistinguished dog.

poppers
An attempt to involve the sinuses in sex or dancing.

POODLE (OBVIOUSLY...)

"post-modern"
The coroner's report on modern. To some, modern with a hangover.

precedents
Posts in the judicial pinball machine.

principle
A rule, inscribed in the core of the universe, which happens to favour my current objective; as, "I think people ought to confront their ageism," translating as: "you, you young whippersnapper/old goat, should be in my bed instead of on your feet."

There's nothing so invincible
as high-and-mighty principle
to make someone convincible
that something rather sensible
is actually indefensible;
that something quite refutable
is really impermutable;
that something simply logical
is merely pedagogical;

that every war in winnable
that every kiss is chinnable
that every room is chintz-able
that every frog is prince-able.

When principles are most purebred
they always lead to war or bed.
— **Emily Postess**

procreation
The production of new Creationists.

promiscuity
A medically unsound activity which transmits indigestion, apoplexy, night sweats, and high blood pressure among large numbers of prudes.

psychiatrist
A mental dentist who attempts to rid you of painful realities. A fitter of mental false teeth.

public
Society's peanut gallery. The public watches everything and does nothing; one becomes a member of the public in watching something one does not do, but ceases to be a member when doing what one does do. It is the inert, mindless collective of active, mindful people. It is a sitcom or soap opera endlessly watching itself with no prospect of ever changing channels.

puritan
Person who believes that worldly pleasure, especially when found in the sexuality, is entirely evil. A human prune struggling to wrinkle itself out of contact with existence. A black hole of human disillusionment.

queer
Word which has been returned by gays to the English language, in exchange for the word "gay." This represents a total saving to the English language of two letters.

RADICAL FAERIE

R

radical fairy
A small, winged creature with insignia on its fuselage. Sometimes referred to in literature as faery, faerie, or faieriee. Tends to excavate clothing of prehistoric women and wear it at ceremonies.

rapist
One-man concentration camp.

Reagan
For many years, the Chief Upholder of the traditional middle-American virtues of parsimony, sanctimoniousness, and belligerence. In his first term of office, Reagan was often strongly criticized for his liason with Bonzo, a chimpanzee, despite the fact that his subsequent taste in friends, allies, and associates was usually much worse.

recruitment
A highly imaginative hypothesis which attempts to account both for the origins of gay men and for the fact that many of them have short hair.

reject (*pronounced REE-ject*)
Someone less appealing than you were the last time you got rejected.

rejection
The art of dodging in mid-tackle; or, the state of being dodged in mid-tackle.

relationship
Liaison usually involving two people and their dirty dishes.

respectable
Familiar with Robert's Rules of Order (as in *respectable gay leader*).

revisionist
Marxist on the road from point A to point B. If isolated, a receptacle for icepicks.

right wing
As with the left wing, half the propulsive force of a flightless bird.

romance
A magical fairy godmother with a prurient gleam in her eye. Although the good fairy can turn a pumpkin into a condominium with ease, she lacks the ability to turn a rat into a noble charger — unless, of course, she induces one to loan the rat one's charge cards. In any event, men should be forewarned not to confuse the emanations of her magic wand with those of their own.

roommate
One member of the obligatory relationship in which compulsively neat individuals and slobs acquire knowledge of each other.

Rorschach
Developer of the famous Ink Blot Test, used for testing sexual normalcy in disturbed squid.

rough trade
Person rendered dangerous to health by possession of three-day-old stubble on chin.

RELATIONSHIP

S

sadomasochism
Power games for fun rather than profit.

San Francisco
Mecca-by-the-Sea, despite the fact that every rainstorm, high wind, and earth tremor is a sign of God's disapproval. City where the Wrong People Vote. A seaport.

> *Red eyes in the morning, sailors take warning.*
> *Red hankie at night, sailor's delight.*
> — **Old San Francisco Rhyme**

scat
Translation of many social transactions into a more literal setting.

self-confessed
Personally revealed despite potential stigma, as, "Mr. Biggs, a homosexual and self-confessed stamp collector"; or "Ms. Jones, a lesbian and self-confessed henna user."

sex
The second-most-intimate human act, next to gossiping.

sexism
Phallocracy; exercise of the Divine Right of Things (as in, "Don't play with that Thing").

sexual harrassment
The bane of working women. Justifies lower wages because constantly antagonized workers produce less.

shock
A politically marketable form of feigned surprise.

sissy
A young boy engaged in any productive activity, e.g. art, cooking, sewing.

size
Length.

sleep
Process thoughtfully provided by evolution in order to pre-empt the need for conversation after sex.

SISSY

small town
A device for close personal surveillance more diabolical than any yet invented by totalitarian regimes.

smut
Literature which sends expectantly quivering conservatives into ecstasies of self-righteousness; hence, a necessary art form which, when not found in pornography, will be found in Shakespeare.

Sodom
A city which was destroyed because its inhabitants were rude. The biblical story of Sodom relates the condemnation of a gang of marauding men who attempted to extort knowledge (or "knowledge") of visitors to the city. Story is often used by Sodomites (rude people) to coerce gays into becoming straight.

Steve
Boyfriend of first gay man. This colourful creation legend is said to have been invented by Rev. Jerry Falwell. The story of how Adam and Steve produced the human race is no more puzzling than the story of where Cain acquired a wife.

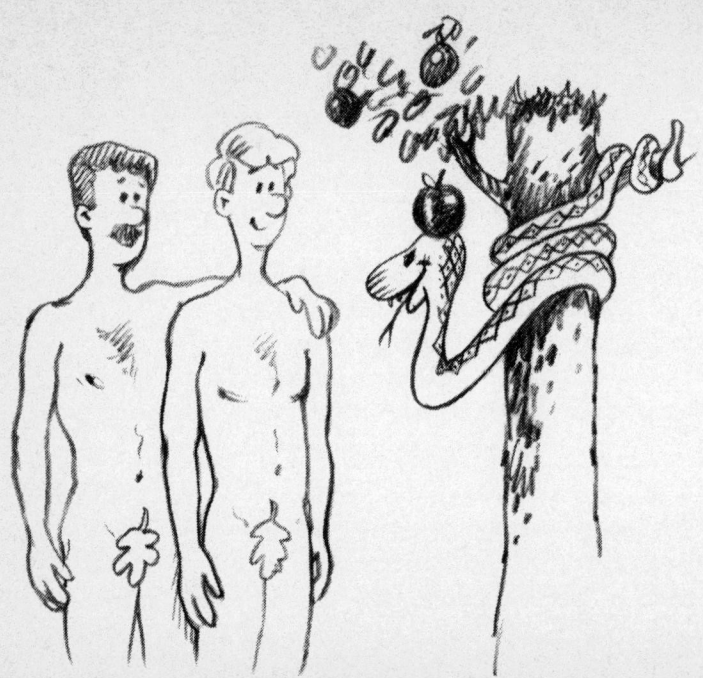

"NO? THEN HOW ABOUT QUICHE INSTEAD?"

ADAM & STEVE

Stonewall Inn
Place where the limp wrist ceased to be a salute to higher authority.

stud
Person distinguished by industrial-strength virility.

sugar daddy
Male cornocupia, or horniness-of-plenty.

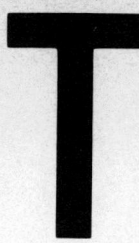

tacky
Not reflecting our own eccentricities, especially in the case of trivial details.

taste
The refined ability to distinguish between the acceptable and the truly repulsive: the virtue of having a stomach which can turn on a dime.

tearoom
A secret meeting place where policemen indulge their most basic urges.

television
The opera of the suburbs. Television has one insuperable advantage over live theatre: you can belch at it.

terrorist
Reprehensible person who fails to wear a uniform while bombing, kidnapping, or assassinating other people.

together
Well-adjusted, serene. Often said of fecal material.

toilet
A bar which you no longer frequent, but which your ex-lover still does.

tomboy
Young girl who gets sufficient exercise.

trashy
Unusually candid, forthright. Trashy bitch: fine, upstanding citizen.

trick
A disappearing act.

Truth
Self-interest.

unhappy
Joyful for the wrong reasons; irreligious. Deserving to be the object of a self-fullfilling prophecy of gloom.

unnatural act
Any everyday human act not equally typical of cattle, sheep, and horses. Singing, smoking, and various heterosexual and homosexual acts are included.

UNNATURAL

V

VD
A form of lightning which regularly strikes twice in the same place. If VD didn't exist, the Roman Catholic church would have to invent it.

vegetarian
Mass-murderer and insatiable devourer of innocent flowers.

VEGETARIAN

water sports
The only known sports not (officially) trained for by East Germans. Situation can be expected to change dramatically if these sports are ever included in the Olympics.

weamaughan
Politically correct spelling of "woman" in Outer Hebrides. The correct spelling of "woman" ("womyn," "wommon," etc.) remains controversial; one feminist group has neatly solved the problem by printing buttons which say "Proud Wo."

wet dream
Youth's initiation into the most fundamental reality of sexual existence: damp sheets.

whore
Man who has a great deal of sex for no money.

wimp
A small derisible, or schleppelin. An apolitical liberal.

x-rated
100% guaranteed prude-free — the most salutary classification in films.

youth
The current fashion in bodily *haut decor* — the world's only lasting fad.
"Acne and cheesecake on drugs."
        — **Milton Murphont,**
        Why I Am Not A
        Pederast

Z

zodiac

Mystic stars that hover somewhere over California. A centuries-old source of Opening Lines, as "Hi, I'm a goat, are you a crab?"

He told me, "You're a Taurus!"
To which I said: "That's Bull."
Said he, "My dear, I know it is,
I'm really not so dull;
and me, now, I'm an Aries!"
"A Ram," I said, "so what?"
He turned and whispered, "Glad you asked:
(I'm famous for my Butt)."

          — Pliny the
          Middle-Aged

AFTERWORD

If you describe things as better than they are, you are considered to be romantic; if you describe things as worse than they are, you will be called a realist; and if you describe things exactly as they are, you will be thought of as a satirist.

— **Quentin Crisp,** *The Naked Civil Servant*